Bug Log

A kid's journal to record their bug discoveries.

This Bug Log belc

D0904618

Special thanks to The Great Bug Creator!

De: I'm grateful to my husband Pete, parents Marilyn and Ralph, kids Mike and Dan, friends Cathy, Jessy, Nancy, JoEllen, and Darrell for their support in life and on this project.

Dan: I'd like to thank my parents for supporting and encouraging me to spend most of my childhood outside, and my brother for joining me in those adventures.

10·9 8 7 6 5 4 3

No part of this book may be reproduced by any means or in any form without the written permission of the publisher.

Published by:
Adventure Publications
An imprint of AdventureKEEN
310 Garfield Street South
Cambridge, Minnesota 55008
(800) 678-7006
www.adventurepublications.net

Printed and bound in China

Cover and interior design/illustration:
DeAnna Brandt, Daniel Brandt
Content: DeAnna Brandt, Daniel Brandt

ISBN 978-1-59193-727-2 (pbk.)

Notice: The information contained in this book is true, complete, and accurate to the best of our knowledge.

All recommendations and suggestions are made without any guarantees on the part of the authors or Adventure Publications.

The authors and publisher disclaim all liability incurred in connection with the use of this information. Neither the publisher nor the authors shall be liable for any damage which may be caused or sustained as a result of the conduct of any of the activities in this book.

Log Tips

Check It Out!

Look up your bug in a nature book, field guide, or on the internet to find out more about it.

Helpful Tools

Bring along this Bug Log and something to write with. A magnifying glass and a camera are both useful, but not necessary.

Record It!

As you explore, write down the bugs you notice on the log pages. Identify what kind of bug it is as mentioned above.

You can record up to 30 bugs on your Life List! Transfer the dates and bug names from those log pages to your Life List pages to create a quick view of your progress.

Be Creative!

Draw directly onto the photos/art pages or attach your original artwork, a photo you've taken, a postcard, or a picture from a magazine.

Have Fun!

Learn more with the bug **Facts**, give back with the **Help** ideas, and explore and play games with the **Nature Play** activities.

Respect Nature!

Please leave bugs as you find them. Observe with your eyes and don't step on or disturb insects, and that includes their homes, such as anthills, beehives, or spiderwebs.

Of course, if you find any unwanted bugs in your home, let your parents know.

Stay Safe!

Some bugs bite or sting. Stay a good distance away from all bugs until you know they cannot harm you. When in doubt, ask an adult first!

Other Uses

You don't have to be outside to use this log. Go to the zoo, natural history museum, science museum, or watch a show on TV or online about bugs.

What's a Bug?

In this Bug Log, we include all sorts of "bugs," from common insects such as beetles, moths, butterflies, bees, flies, and ants to other "creepy crawlies" such as spiders, earthworms, and more. This helps us include all of the familiar insects you expect as well as some of the other, lesser-known critters that are found in nature.

All of the animals listed above— with the exception of worms— are known as **Arthropods**, a big group of animals that includes insects, spiders, scorpions, centipedes, and even some crustaceans, such as ticks, mites, and even shrimp. An arthropod is an animal with a hard exoskeleton, segmented bodies, and jointed legs.

Insects are the largest group of arthropods. They have a hard outside body covering called an exoskeleton, and they have three body sections—a head, a thorax, and an abdomen. Their heads have two antennae, and they have three pairs of legs linked to their thorax. Many can also fly with one or two pairs of wings.

In the United States, scientists have described about 91,000 insect species, but according to one estimate, there are maybe 70,000 other insect species to be described. Worldwide, scientists estimate that there may be millions of other insect species.

Earthworms are segmented worms and belong to a group known as **Annelids**. We've included them here because people sometimes mistake them for insects.

Bug Parts

If you know the different parts of a bug, it's easier to identify it. These illustrations show the basic parts of two insects.

ANT

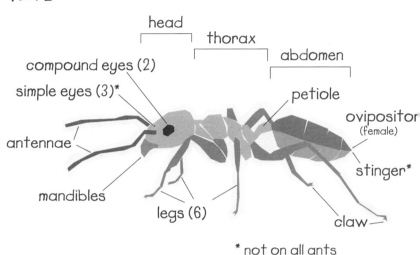

head

thorax

abdomen

compound eyes (2)

simple eyes (3)*

petiole

ovipositor
(female)

antennae

stinger*

mandibles

legs (6)

claw

* not on all ants

GRASSHOPPER

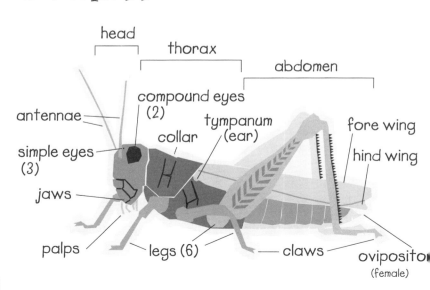

head

thorax

abdomen

compound eyes
(2)

tympanum
(ear)

antennae

collar

fore wing

simple eyes
(3)

hind wing

jaws

palps

legs (6)

claws

ovipositor
(female)

Bug Parts

These illustrations show the basic parts of a worm and a spider (both are technically not insects).

EARTHWORM

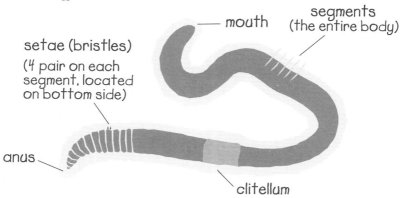

setae (bristles)
(4 pair on each segment, located on bottom side)

mouth

segments
(the entire body)

anus

clitellum

Fun Fact: I have 5 hearts inside my body!

SPIDER

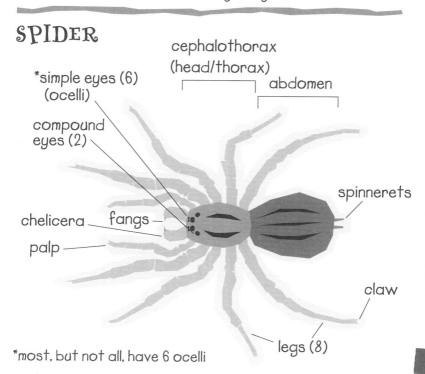

*simple eyes (6)
(ocelli)

compound
eyes (2)

cephalothorax
(head/thorax)

abdomen

spinnerets

chelicera

fangs

palp

claw

legs (8)

*most, but not all, have 6 ocelli

Life Cycle

Have you ever wondered how a caterpillar becomes a butterfly? It gets there through **metamorphosis**, a series of changes in an insect's appearance and structure over time. About 85 percent of insects go through a 4-stage cycle called **complete metamorphosis,** starting out from an egg, turning into a larva, then a pupa, and finally emerging as an adult. This includes butterflies and moths, beetles, ants, wasps, bees, and flies. Other bugs go through a 3-stage process called **incomplete metamorphosis**. They start as an egg, turn into a larva, and become an adult. Dragonflies, cockroaches, grasshoppers, praying mantises, crickets, and walking sticks all have a 3-stage metamorphosis.

Butterfly Metamorphosis

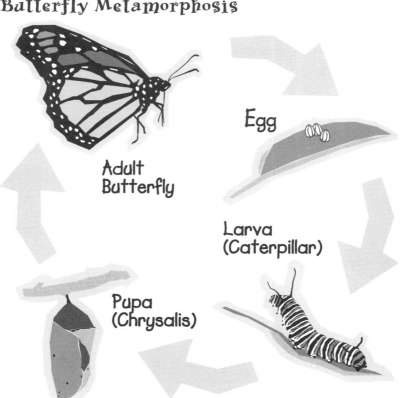

Adult Butterfly

Egg

Larva (Caterpillar)

Pupa (Chrysalis)

State Bugs

45 States in the U.S. have chosen a "state insect." Some of them also have a "state butterfly" and more! Check out your own state below.

Alabama
Monarch Butterfly

Alaska
Four-Spotted Skimmer
Dragonfly

Arizona
Two-Tailed Swallowtail

Arkansas
European Honeybee
Diana Fritillary Butterfly

California
California Dogface Butterfly

Colorado
Colorado Hairstreak
Butterfly

Connecticut
European Mantis

Delaware
7-Spotted Ladybug

Florida
Zebra Longwing

Georgia
European Honeybee
Eastern Tiger Swallowtail

Hawaii
Kamehameha Butterfly

Idaho
Monarch Butterfly

Illinois
Monarch Butterfly

Kansas
European Honeybee

Kentucky
Viceroy Butterfly

Louisiana
European Honeybee

Maine
European Honeybee

Maryland
Baltimore Checkerspot
Butterfly

Massachusetts
7-Spotted Ladybug

Minnesota
Monarch Butterfly

Mississippi
European Honeybee
Spicebush Swallowtail

Missouri
European Honeybee

Montana
Mourning Cloak Butterfly

Nebraska
European Honeybee

New Hampshire
7-Spotted Ladybug
Karner Blue Butterfly

New Jersey
European Honeybee

New Mexico
Tarantula Hawk Wasp
Sandia Hairstreak Butterfly

New York
9-Spotted Ladybug

North Carolina
European Honeybee
Eastern Tiger Swallowtail

North Dakota
Convergent Lady Beetle

Ohio
7-Spotted Ladybug

Oklahoma
European Honeybee
Black Swallowtail Butterfly

Oregon
Oregon Swallowtail
Butterfly

Pennsylvania
Pennsylvania Firefly

Rhode Island
American Burying Beetle

South Carolina
Carolina Mantis
Eastern Tiger Swallowtail

South Dakota
European Honeybee

Tennessee
Common Eastern Firefly
7-Spotted Ladybug
European Honeybee
Zebra Swallowtail
Butterfly

Texas
Monarch Butterfly

Utah
European Honeybee

Vermont
European Honeybee
Monarch Butterfly

Virginia
Eastern Tiger Swallowtail
Butterfly

Washington
Green Darner Dragonfly

West Virginia
European Honeybee
Monarch Butterfly

Wisconsin
European Honeybee

Wyoming
Sheridan's Green
Hairstreak

Common Words

Abdomen: The end part of a spider's body. Also the end part of an insect's body, joined to its thorax.

Antennae: A pair of long skinny parts on the head of insects and other arthropods. They are often the critter's "nose" and used for smelling; they are also used for touching.

Arachnids: A group of arthropods that includes spiders, mites, ticks, scorpions, and harvestmen (daddy long legs). **Note:** Even though such animals are often considered insects, they're not. They are arthropods.

Arthropod: Invertebrate animals that have jointed legs, an exoskeleton, and a segmented body. About 85 percent of all known animals in the world are arthropods.

Beetles (Coleoptera): The largest category of insects, which includes ladybird beetles, scarabs, and fireflies. About 40 percent of all known insect species are beetles; there are about 400,000 beetle species in the world with about 25,000 in North America.

Biological Control: Human use of a living organism to control another pesky one. For example, people use ladybugs in their gardens to eat the aphids that can ruin plants.

Carnivore: An animal that eats other animals. Dragonflies and praying mantises are carnivores.

Compound Eye: The main eye in insects and other arthropods. There are thousands of lenses in each eye, making it look like a pattern of tiny balls.

Conservation: Protecting things found in nature.

Drone: A male bee (like a honeybee) that only mates with the queen, has no stinger, and does not gather pollen or nectar.

Exoskeleton: An outer casing that protects and supports an animal's body.

Common Words

Frass: An insect larva's poop.

Glossa: An insect's tongue.

Habitat: Where an animal or plant lives.

Herbivore: An animal that only eats plants. Butterflies are herbivores; they only drink nectar from plants.

Invertebrate: Animals without a backbone. Corals, insects, worms, jellyfish, starfish, and snails are invertebrates. More than 96 percent of all the animals on the planet are invertebrates.

Omnivore: Animals that eat plants and other animals.

Pollen Basket: The pollen-collecting area on honeybees and bumblebees; it is located on their hind legs and made of short hairs that surround an indented spot on their legs.

Pollination: The process of moving pollen from one plant to another plant. Bees do this all the time as they visit different plants and flowers.

Proboscis: The long, tubular feeding and sucking part of butterflies and mosquitoes.

Stinger: The pointed part of an insect that can inject poison and can be painful or dangerous. Scorpions, bees, ants, and wasps all have a stinger.

Stridulation: The act of producing sound, usually by rubbing two body parts together. Crickets are famous for this.

Venom: The poisonous liquid produced by an animal, such as a spider or a scorpion, that is used to kill prey or fight off predators. Usually delivered with a bite or a sting.

Life List

	Date	Bug Name
1	_____	_____
2	_____	_____
3	_____	_____
4	_____	_____
5	_____	_____
6	_____	_____
7	_____	_____
8	_____	_____
9	_____	_____
10	_____	_____
11	_____	_____
12	_____	_____
13	_____	_____
14	_____	_____
15	_____	_____

Life List

Date	Bug Name
16	
17	
18	
19	
20	
21	
22	
23	
24	
25	
26	
27	
28	
29	
30	

Log

Date/Time: _____

Season: _____

Weather Conditions: _____

Bug Location: ☐ ground ☐ tree ☐ air
☐ under log/rock ☐ other _____

What is it doing? _____
_____

How many are there? _____

Do you see: ☐ eggs ☐ larvae ☐ nest/home
Describe: _____
_____

What shape/size is it? _____

How many legs? ☐ 6 ☐ 8 ☐ other _____

If you can see eyes, what do they look like?
☐ compound (many) ☐ simple ☐ other _____

Any wings? If so, are they: (check all that apply)
☐ mostly clear ☐ solid ☐ plain ☐ colorful
Colors: _____

Any antennae? Describe: _____

Special markings? _____

What colors are on it (other than its wings)?
_____

Name of bug I saw (enter this on your Life List)

Does it make a sound? If so, it makes a:
(circle all that apply) squeak hiss click
crackle buzz song creak chirp whir hum
Other_____

Other interesting things I noticed:

_____
_____
_____
_____
_____
_____
_____

It looks like this: (drawing or photo)

Fact

Bombardier Beetles are small beetles with a red head and legs and blue wing coverings. More than 40 species are found in the United States.

They are unique because they can shoot poisonous, stinky, boiling-hot chemicals from their abdomens onto predators. The built-in spray tip on their bodies can aim almost anywhere—even over their own backs!

13

Log

Date/Time: _____

Season: _____

Weather Conditions: _____

Bug Location: ☐ ground ☐ tree ☐ air
☐ under log/rock ☐ other_____

What is it doing? _____
_____

How many are there? _____

Do you see: ☐ eggs ☐ larvae ☐ nest/home
Describe: _____
_____

What shape/size is it?_____

How many legs? ☐ 6 ☐ 8 ☐ other _____

If you can see eyes, what do they look like?
☐ compound (many) ☐ simple ☐ other _____

Any wings? If so, are they: (check all that apply)
☐ mostly clear ☐ solid ☐ plain ☐ colorful
Colors: _____

Any antennae? Describe: _____

Special markings? _____

What colors are on it (other than its wings)?
_____

Name of bug I saw (enter this on your Life List)

Does it make a sound? If so, it makes a: (circle all that apply) squeak hiss click crackle buzz song creak chirp whir hum Other_____

Other interesting things I noticed:

_____

_____

_____

_____

_____

_____

_____

It looks like this: (drawing or photo)

Fact

How far can you jump? The world record for the long jump is 29 feet, 4 ½ inches; it was set by Mike Powell, an American athlete, in 1991.

The best jumpers in the insect world are the froghoppers, which can jump more than 2 feet, despite being only ¼ of an inch long. Not bad!

3

Log

Date/Time: _____

Season: _____

Weather Conditions: _____

Bug Location: ☐ ground ☐ tree ☐ air
☐ under log/rock ☐ other_____

What is it doing? _____
_____

How many are there? _____

Do you see: ☐ eggs ☐ larvae ☐ nest/home
Describe: _____
_____

What shape/size is it?_____

How many legs? ☐ 6 ☐ 8 ☐ other _____

If you can see eyes, what do they look like?
☐ compound (many) ☐ simple ☐ other _____

Any wings? If so, are they: (check all that apply)
☐ mostly clear ☐ solid ☐ plain ☐ colorful
Colors: _____

Any antennae? Describe: _____

Special markings? _____

What colors are on it (other than its wings)?
_____

Name of bug I saw (enter this on your Life List)

Does it make a sound? If so, it makes a: (circle all that apply) squeak hiss click crackle buzz song creak chirp whir hum Other_____

Other interesting things I noticed:

_____

_____

_____

_____

_____

_____

_____

It looks like this: (drawing or photo)

Fact

When it comes to insect bites and stings, mosquitoes are, far and away, the most dangerous insects (and animals!) in the world. Why? They carry diseases, such as malaria, that kill millions of people each year.

But which insect has the strongest bite? That might just be the Titan Beetle, which has jaws powerful enough to snap plastic rulers or pencils.

4

Log

Date/Time: _____

Season: _____

Weather Conditions: _____

Bug Location: ☐ ground ☐ tree ☐ air
☐ under log/rock ☐ other_____

What is it doing? _____
_____

How many are there? _____

Do you see: ☐ eggs ☐ larvae ☐ nest/home
Describe: _____
_____

What shape/size is it? _____

How many legs? ☐ 6 ☐ 8 ☐ other _____

If you can see eyes, what do they look like?
☐ compound (many) ☐ simple ☐ other _____

Any wings? If so, are they: (check all that apply)
☐ mostly clear ☐ solid ☐ plain ☐ colorful
Colors: _____

Any antennae? Describe: _____

Special markings? _____

What colors are on it (other than its wings)?
_____

Name of bug I saw (enter this on your Life List)

Does it make a sound? If so, it makes a: (circle all that apply) squeak hiss click crackle buzz song creak chirp whir hum Other_____

Other interesting things I noticed:

_____
_____
_____
_____
_____
_____
_____

It looks like this: (drawing or photo)

Activity

Using clay, mud, dirt, or sand, make your own bug. You might use sticks for legs, seeds for eyes, leaves for wings, or whatever you like. This is your own creation, so it doesn't have to be realistic. If it's a bug that crawls, figure out how many legs it has. If it flies, give it wings. It can be small, medium, or super-size. And when you're done, give it a name!

Take a picture of it and print it out. Attach it to the Photo Page of this Log.

Log

Date/Time: _____

Season: _____

Weather Conditions: _____

Bug Location: ☐ ground ☐ tree ☐ air
☐ under log/rock ☐ other_____

What is it doing? _____
_____

How many are there? _____

Do you see: ☐ eggs ☐ larvae ☐ nest/home
Describe: _____
_____

What shape/size is it?_____

How many legs? ☐ 6 ☐ 8 ☐ other _____

If you can see eyes, what do they look like?
☐ compound (many) ☐ simple ☐ other ____

Any wings? If so, are they: (check all that apply)
☐ mostly clear ☐ solid ☐ plain ☐ colorful
Colors: _____

Any antennae? Describe: _____

Special markings? _____

What colors are on it (other than its wings)?
_____

Name of bug I saw (enter this on your Life List)

Does it make a sound? If so, it makes a: (circle all that apply) squeak hiss click crackle buzz song creak chirp whir hum Other_____

Other interesting things I noticed:

_____
_____
_____
_____
_____
_____

It looks like this: (drawing or photo)

Fact

Many animals, insects included, try to avoid being seen by predators. That's why many are drab browns or greens. They don't want to be found; if they are, they might get munched!

That's not the case with some insects, though. Monarch Butterflies are brightly colored. Why? They're poisonous and they want potential predators to know it and stay away!

 Log

Date/Time: _____

Season: _____

Weather Conditions: _____

Bug Location: ☐ ground ☐ tree ☐ air
☐ under log/rock ☐ other_____

What is it doing? _____
_____

How many are there? _____

Do you see: ☐ eggs ☐ larvae ☐ nest/home
Describe: _____
_____

What shape/size is it?_____

How many legs? ☐ 6 ☐ 8 ☐ other _____

If you can see eyes, what do they look like?
☐ compound (many) ☐ simple ☐ other _____

Any wings? If so, are they: (check all that apply)
☐ mostly clear ☐ solid ☐ plain ☐ colorful
Colors: _____

Any antennae? Describe: _____

Special markings? _____

What colors are on it (other than its wings)?
_____

Name of bug I saw (enter this on your Life List)

Does it make a sound? If so, it makes a:
(circle all that apply) squeak hiss click
crackle buzz song creak chirp whir hum
Other_____

Other interesting things I noticed:

_____
_____
_____
_____
_____
_____
_____

It looks like this: (drawing or photo)

Fact

Some insects can fly really fast. The fastest bug on record is a dragonfly from Australia called the Southern Giant Darner, which reaches speeds of up to 60 miles an hour.

There might be other bugs out there that are faster, though; one researcher claims to have recorded a bug belonging to the horsefly family racing at 90 miles per hour!

 Log

Date/Time: _____

Season: _____

Weather Conditions: _____

Bug Location: ☐ ground ☐ tree ☐ air
☐ under log/rock ☐ other_____

What is it doing? _____
_____

How many are there? _____

Do you see: ☐ eggs ☐ larvae ☐ nest/home
Describe: _____
_____

What shape/size is it? _____

How many legs? ☐ 6 ☐ 8 ☐ other _____

If you can see eyes, what do they look like?
☐ compound (many) ☐ simple ☐ other _____

Any wings? If so, are they: (check all that apply)
☐ mostly clear ☐ solid ☐ plain ☐ colorful
Colors: _____

Any antennae? Describe: _____

Special markings? _____

What colors are on it (other than its wings)?
_____

Does it make a sound? If so, it makes a:
(circle all that apply) squeak hiss click
crackle buzz song creak chirp whir hum
Other_____

Other interesting things I noticed:

_____
_____
_____
_____
_____
_____
_____

It looks like this: (drawing or photo)

Fact

The Atlas Moth is one of the largest insects alive today; its wings can be up to 11 inches wide! If you want to see the biggest insect of all time, you'll need a time machine. That title belongs to *Meganeura*, a dragonfly that lived 250 million years ago. It had a wingspan that was more than two feet wide!

Log

Date/Time: _____

Season: _____

Weather Conditions: _____

Bug Location: ☐ ground ☐ tree ☐ air
☐ under log/rock ☐ other_____

What is it doing? _____
_____

How many are there? _____

Do you see: ☐ eggs ☐ larvae ☐ nest/home
Describe: _____
_____

What shape/size is it?_____

How many legs? ☐ 6 ☐ 8 ☐ other ____

If you can see eyes, what do they look like?
☐ compound (many) ☐ simple ☐ other ____

Any wings? If so, are they: (check all that apply)
☐ mostly clear ☐ solid ☐ plain ☐ colorful
Colors: _____

Any antennae? Describe: _____

Special markings? _____

What colors are on it (other than its wings)?
_____

Name of bug I saw (enter this on your Life List)

Does it make a sound? If so, it makes a: (circle all that apply) squeak hiss click crackle buzz song creak chirp whir hum Other_____

Other interesting things I noticed:

_____
_____
_____
_____
_____
_____
_____

It looks like this: (drawing or photo)

Help

Go outside or imagine you are walking down the road or a trail. What do you see that would impact bugs (trash, a squashed anthill, flowers that are full of bugs, a sign telling you the yard is sprayed with chemicals, a squished bug, etc.)?

How will these impact bugs?

What could you do to help create a more positive impact? How can you help bugs and other wildlife?

Log

Date/Time: _____

Season: _____

Weather Conditions: _____

Bug Location: ☐ ground ☐ tree ☐ air
☐ under log/rock ☐ other_____

What is it doing? _____
_____

How many are there? _____

Do you see: ☐ eggs ☐ larvae ☐ nest/home
Describe: _____
_____

What shape/size is it?_____

How many legs? ☐ 6 ☐ 8 ☐ other _____

If you can see eyes, what do they look like?
☐ compound (many) ☐ simple ☐ other _____

Any wings? If so, are they: (check all that apply)
☐ mostly clear ☐ solid ☐ plain ☐ colorful
Colors: _____

Any antennae? Describe: _____

Special markings? _____

What colors are on it (other than its wings)?
_____

Name of bug I saw (enter this on your Life List)

Does it make a sound? If so, it makes a: (circle all that apply) squeak hiss click crackle buzz song creak chirp whir hum Other_____

Other interesting things I noticed:

_____

_____

_____

_____

_____

_____

_____

It looks like this: (drawing or photo)

Fact

Tiger beetles are the fastest known beetles on the planet. At less than $1/2$ inch long, they can run almost 6 miles per hour.

In fact, they can run so fast that their eyes can't gather enough light, causing their sharp vision to blur. This means they often have to stop a couple times before actually capturing their prey, but this doesn't matter, as they can just sprint again to catch it!

Log

Date/Time: _____

Season: _____

Weather Conditions: _____

Bug Location: ☐ ground　☐ tree　☐ air
☐ under log/rock　☐ other_____

What is it doing? _____
_____

How many are there? _____

Do you see: ☐ eggs　☐ larvae　☐ nest/home
Describe: _____
_____

What shape/size is it?_____

How many legs?　☐ 6　☐ 8　☐ other _____

If you can see eyes, what do they look like?
☐ compound (many)　☐ simple　☐ other _____

Any wings? If so, are they: (check all that apply)
☐ mostly clear　☐ solid　☐ plain　☐ colorful
Colors: _____

Any antennae? Describe: _____

Special markings? _____

What colors are on it (other than its wings)?
_____

Name of bug I saw (enter this on your Life List)

Does it make a sound? If so, it makes a: (circle all that apply) squeak hiss click crackle buzz song creak chirp whir hum Other_____

Other interesting things I noticed:

_____
_____
_____
_____
_____
_____
_____

It looks like this: (drawing or photo)

Fact

A colony of invasive ants in California runs along the coast-line for more than 550 miles. The ants are native to Argentina in South America and are known as Argentine ants. They are now found in many countries around the world. Amazingly, each Argentine ant can recognize other members of it species, even those from anywhere in the world, making them all part of one big family, and the largest group of animals on the planet.

Log

Date/Time: _____

Season: _____

Weather Conditions: _____

Bug Location: ☐ ground   ☐ tree   ☐ air
☐ under log/rock   ☐ other_____

What is it doing? _____
_____

How many are there? _____

Do you see: ☐ eggs ☐ larvae ☐ nest/home
Describe: _____
_____

What shape/size is it?_____

How many legs?   ☐ 6   ☐ 8   ☐ other _____

If you can see eyes, what do they look like?
☐ compound (many) ☐ simple ☐ other _____

Any wings? If so, are they: (check all that apply)
☐ mostly clear ☐ solid ☐ plain ☐ colorful
Colors: _____

Any antennae? Describe: _____

Special markings? _____

What colors are on it (other than its wings)?
_____

Name of bug I saw (enter this on your Life List)

Does it make a sound? If so, it makes a: (circle all that apply) squeak hiss click crackle buzz song creak chirp whir hum
Other_____

Other interesting things I noticed:

_____
_____
_____
_____
_____
_____

It looks like this: (drawing or photo)

Fact

According to one study, there may be upwards of 400 million individual insects per acre of land in some places.

That means there are more insects in one acre than people in the United States. According to the Smithsonian Institution, there may be 10 quintillion individual insects alive at one time, meaning there may be more than one billion insects for each person on Earth.

Log

Date/Time: _____

Season: _____

Weather Conditions: _____

Bug Location: ☐ ground　☐ tree　☐ air
☐ under log/rock　☐ other_____

What is it doing? _____
_____

How many are there?_____

Do you see: ☐ eggs ☐ larvae ☐ nest/home
Describe: _____
_____

What shape/size is it?_____

How many legs?　☐ 6　☐ 8　☐ other _____

If you can see eyes, what do they look like?
☐ compound (many) ☐ simple ☐ other _____

Any wings? If so, are they: (check all that apply)
☐ mostly clear　☐ solid ☐ plain ☐ colorful
Colors: _____

Any antennae? Describe: _____

Special markings? _____

What colors are on it (other than its wings)?
_____

Name of bug I saw (enter this on your Life List)

Does it make a sound? If so, it makes a:
(circle all that apply) squeak hiss click
crackle buzz song creak chirp whir hum
Other_____

Other interesting things I noticed:

_____
_____
_____
_____
_____
_____
_____

It looks like this: (drawing or photo)

Activity

Pretend you are a bug for a day. You can be a spider, a butterfly, a worm, whatever you'd like.

Imagine your day from the beginning to end. How do you go about finding food, avoiding being eaten, finding or building shelter? What animals do you see? What are they doing? How do you interact with them? Do you swim in the water or run alongside it? Do you crawl on the ground or fly up a tree? What do you see from there? Do you make a sound? Why? Write the story down and include it in this Log.

Log

Date/Time: _____

Season: _____

Weather Conditions: _____

Bug Location: ☐ ground   ☐ tree   ☐ air
☐ under log/rock   ☐ other_____

What is it doing? _____
_____

How many are there? _____

Do you see: ☐ eggs   ☐ larvae   ☐ nest/home
Describe: _____
_____

What shape/size is it?_____

How many legs?   ☐ 6   ☐ 8   ☐ other _____

If you can see eyes, what do they look like?
☐ compound (many) ☐ simple ☐ other _____

Any wings? If so, are they: (check all that apply)
☐ mostly clear ☐ solid ☐ plain ☐ colorful
Colors: _____

Any antennae? Describe: _____

Special markings? _____

What colors are on it (other than its wings)?
_____

Name of bug I saw (enter this on your Life List)

Does it make a sound? If so, it makes a: (circle all that apply) squeak hiss click crackle buzz song creak chirp whir hum Other_____

Other interesting things I noticed:

_____
_____
_____
_____
_____
_____
_____

It looks like this: (drawing or photo)

Fact

Queen Alexandra's Birdwing is the largest butterfly in the world. Its wingspan can reach almost 10 inches!

Unfortunately for butterfly fans, it's also one of the rarest butterflies on the planet, found only in one province of Papua New Guinea. It is now endangered because the old-growth forests it depends upon to survive are threatened.

Log

Date/Time: _____

Season: _____

Weather Conditions: _____

Bug Location: ☐ ground   ☐ tree   ☐ air
☐ under log/rock   ☐ other_____

What is it doing? _____
_____

How many are there?_____

Do you see: ☐ eggs ☐ larvae ☐ nest/home
Describe: _____
_____

What shape/size is it?_____

How many legs?   ☐ 6   ☐ 8   ☐ other _____

If you can see eyes, what do they look like?
☐ compound (many) ☐ simple ☐ other _____

Any wings? If so, are they: (check all that apply)
☐ mostly clear   ☐ solid ☐ plain   ☐ colorful
Colors: _____

Any antennae? Describe: _____

Special markings? _____

What colors are on it (other than its wings)?
_____

Does it make a sound? If so, it makes a: (circle all that apply) squeak hiss click crackle buzz song creak chirp whir hum Other_____

Other interesting things I noticed:

_____
_____
_____
_____
_____
_____

It looks like this: (drawing or photo)

Fact

How do Fireflies light up? They're flying chemistry labs! They mix a special combination of chemicals together inside their bodies and it creates light!

They light up for two main reasons: to signal to a mate, and to advertise the fact that they are toxic. You read that right, fireflies are toxic, at least to their would-be predators, so lighting up helps keep them from becoming lunch!

Log

Date/Time: _____

Season: _____

Weather Conditions: _____

Bug Location: ☐ ground ☐ tree ☐ air
☐ under log/rock ☐ other _____

What is it doing? _____
_____

How many are there? _____

Do you see: ☐ eggs ☐ larvae ☐ nest/home
Describe: _____
_____

What shape/size is it? _____

How many legs? ☐ 6 ☐ 8 ☐ other _____

If you can see eyes, what do they look like?
☐ compound (many) ☐ simple ☐ other _____

Any wings? If so, are they: (check all that apply)
☐ mostly clear ☐ solid ☐ plain ☐ colorful
Colors: _____

Any antennae? Describe: _____

Special markings? _____

What colors are on it (other than its wings)?
_____

Does it make a sound? If so, it makes a:
(circle all that apply) squeak hiss click
crackle buzz song creak chirp whir hum
Other_____

Other interesting things I noticed:

_____
_____
_____
_____
_____
_____
_____

It looks like this: (drawing or photo)

Fact

Some bees make honey. It takes thousands of bees and about two million flowers to produce just a pound of honey, and bees often have to travel for a mile or more to find the flowers.

When they do, they tell their friends by dancing. This "waggle dance" helps them know the direction to travel to find food and uses the sun as a reference point.

 Log

Date/Time: _____

Season: _____

Weather Conditions: _____

Bug Location: ☐ ground ☐ tree ☐ air
☐ under log/rock ☐ other_____

What is it doing? _____
_____

How many are there? _____

Do you see: ☐ eggs ☐ larvae ☐ nest/home
Describe: _____
_____

What shape/size is it?_____

How many legs? ☐ 6 ☐ 8 ☐ other _____

If you can see eyes, what do they look like?
☐ compound (many) ☐ simple ☐ other ____

Any wings? If so, are they: (check all that apply)
☐ mostly clear ☐ solid ☐ plain ☐ colorful
Colors: _____

Any antennae? Describe: _____

Special markings? _____

What colors are on it (other than its wings)?
_____

Name of bug I saw (enter this on your Life List)

Does it make a sound? If so, it makes a:
(circle all that apply) squeak hiss click
crackle buzz song creak chirp whir hum
Other_____

Other interesting things I noticed:

_____
_____
_____
_____
_____
_____

It looks like this: (drawing or photo)

Help

In a container outside, or in your yard, make a bug-friendly zone by planting something that helps bees and butterflies.

There are many options to choose from and you can look them up online or go to a garden center and find out what would work in your climate.

Learn which plants are good for the bees and butterflies and try to grow different plants each year. Pretty soon, you'll have lots of buzzing visitors!

Log

Date/Time: _____

Season: _____

Weather Conditions: _____

Bug Location: ☐ ground ☐ tree ☐ air
☐ under log/rock ☐ other _____

What is it doing? _____
_____

How many are there? _____

Do you see: ☐ eggs ☐ larvae ☐ nest/home
Describe: _____
_____

What shape/size is it? _____

How many legs? ☐ 6 ☐ 8 ☐ other _____

If you can see eyes, what do they look like?
☐ compound (many) ☐ simple ☐ other _____

Any wings? If so, are they: (check all that apply)
☐ mostly clear ☐ solid ☐ plain ☐ colorful
Colors: _____

Any antennae? Describe: _____

Special markings? _____

What colors are on it (other than its wings)?
_____

Name of bug I saw (enter this on your Life List)

Does it make a sound? If so, it makes a: (circle all that apply) squeak hiss click crackle buzz song creak chirp whir hum

Other_____

Other interesting things I noticed:

_____
_____
_____
_____
_____
_____
_____

It looks like this: (drawing or photo)

Fact

In the United States, there are about 200 different kinds of ticks. They live in tall grass, bushes, leaf piles, and wooded areas. They can climb up and hang out on those structures and wait until a human or another animal passes. Then, they drop onto their new host. They cannot fly or jump, but they may fall from their lookout spot.

Always avoid ticks; they spread serious diseases that can affect people and pets.

Log

Date/Time: _____

Season: _____

Weather Conditions: _____

Bug Location: ☐ ground ☐ tree ☐ air
☐ under log/rock ☐ other _____

What is it doing? _____
_____

How many are there? _____

Do you see: ☐ eggs ☐ larvae ☐ nest/home
Describe: _____
_____

What shape/size is it? _____

How many legs? ☐ 6 ☐ 8 ☐ other _____

If you can see eyes, what do they look like?
☐ compound (many) ☐ simple ☐ other _____

Any wings? If so, are they: (check all that apply)
☐ mostly clear ☐ solid ☐ plain ☐ colorful
Colors: _____

Any antennae? Describe: _____

Special markings? _____

What colors are on it (other than its wings)?
_____

Does it make a sound? If so, it makes a:
(circle all that apply) squeak hiss click
crackle buzz song creak chirp whir hum
Other_____

Other interesting things I noticed:

_____
_____
_____
_____
_____
_____
_____

It looks like this: (drawing or photo)

Fact

Dragonflies are the predators of the insect world. While we admire them for their grace in the air and ability to hover, fly backward, and change direction at high speed, other flying insects fear them. Why? Simple: they don't want to become lunch.

Dragonflies thrive because of their ability to eat other flying insects, and they do this by streaking through the air like a fighter plane and snatching other bugs out of the sky.

Log

Date/Time: _____

Season: _____

Weather Conditions: _____

Bug Location: ☐ ground ☐ tree ☐ air
☐ under log/rock ☐ other _____

What is it doing? _____
_____

How many are there? _____

Do you see: ☐ eggs ☐ larvae ☐ nest/home
Describe: _____
_____

What shape/size is it? _____

How many legs? ☐ 6 ☐ 8 ☐ other ____

If you can see eyes, what do they look like?
☐ compound (many) ☐ simple ☐ other ____

Any wings? If so, are they: (check all that apply)
☐ mostly clear ☐ solid ☐ plain ☐ colorful
Colors: _____

Any antennae? Describe: _____

Special markings? _____

What colors are on it (other than its wings)?
_____

Name of bug I saw (enter this on your Life List)

Does it make a sound? If so, it makes a: (circle all that apply) squeak hiss click crackle buzz song creak chirp whir hum Other_____

Fact

Some scientists and engineers study winged insects to see exactly how they fly.

Studying bug wings and muscles could be used to make better drones, or flying robots.

Other interesting things I noticed:

_____
_____
_____
_____
_____
_____
_____

It looks like this: (drawing or photo)

Log

Date/Time: _____

Season: _____

Weather Conditions: _____

Bug Location: ☐ ground   ☐ tree   ☐ air
☐ under log/rock   ☐ other_____

What is it doing? _____
_____

How many are there? _____

Do you see: ☐ eggs ☐ larvae ☐ nest/home
Describe: _____
_____

What shape/size is it?_____

How many legs?   ☐ 6   ☐ 8   ☐ other _____

If you can see eyes, what do they look like?
☐ compound (many) ☐ simple ☐ other _____

Any wings? If so, are they: (check all that apply)
☐ mostly clear   ☐ solid ☐ plain ☐ colorful
Colors: _____

Any antennae? Describe: _____

Special markings? _____

What colors are on it (other than its wings)?
_____

Does it make a sound? If so, it makes a:
(circle all that apply) squeak hiss click
crackle buzz song creak chirp whir hum
Other_____

Other interesting things I noticed:

_____
_____
_____
_____
_____
_____
_____

It looks like this: (drawing or photo)

Activity

With a piece of paper (4"x6" or less) and a pencil/pen, go outside and find a bug.

Observe the shapes and patterns on it. Circles, ovals, straight or curvy lines, and stripes can all be found on various bugs.

Use ONLY the shapes and patterns you see on that bug to create a new drawing. (It doesn't have to be a bug). Sign your artwork and attach it to the Photo/Art page of this log.

Log

Date/Time: _____

Season: _____

Weather Conditions: _____

Bug Location: ☐ ground ☐ tree ☐ air
☐ under log/rock ☐ other_____

What is it doing? _____
_____

How many are there? _____

Do you see: ☐ eggs ☐ larvae ☐ nest/home
Describe: _____
_____

What shape/size is it?_____

How many legs? ☐ 6 ☐ 8 ☐ other _____

If you can see eyes, what do they look like?
☐ compound (many) ☐ simple ☐ other _____

Any wings? If so, are they: (check all that apply)
☐ mostly clear ☐ solid ☐ plain ☐ colorful
Colors: _____

Any antennae? Describe: _____

Special markings? _____

What colors are on it (other than its wings)?
_____

Name of bug I saw (enter this on your Life List)

Does it make a sound? If so, it makes a:
(circle all that apply) squeak hiss click
crackle buzz song creak chirp whir hum
Other_____

Other interesting things I noticed:

_____
_____
_____
_____
_____
_____
_____

It looks like this: (drawing or photo)

Fact

Beetles are the largest group of insects, with about 400,000 different species discovered so far. In fact, they are the largest group of animals on the planet; 1 in 4 animals on Earth is a beetle. If aliens discovered Earth, they might say it was largely inhabited by beetles, and with a small human population.

Log

Date/Time: _____

Season: _____

Weather Conditions: _____

Bug Location: ☐ ground ☐ tree ☐ air
☐ under log/rock ☐ other_____

What is it doing? _____
_____

How many are there?_____

Do you see: ☐ eggs ☐ larvae ☐ nest/home
Describe: _____
_____

What shape/size is it?_____

How many legs? ☐ 6 ☐ 8 ☐ other _____

If you can see eyes, what do they look like?
☐ compound (many) ☐ simple ☐ other _____

Any wings? If so, are they: (check all that apply)
☐ mostly clear ☐ solid ☐ plain ☐ colorful
Colors: _____

Any antennae? Describe: _____

Special markings? _____

What colors are on it (other than its wings)?
_____

Name of bug I saw (enter this on your Life List)

Does it make a sound? If so, it makes a: (circle all that apply) squeak hiss click crackle buzz song creak chirp whir hum Other_____

Other interesting things I noticed:

_____
_____
_____
_____
_____
_____
_____

It looks like this: (drawing or photo)

Fact

Scientists have discovered more than 14,000 different kinds of ants, with new ones being found continually.

For every human on earth, there are about 1 million ants; if you want to find the most ants, head to the Amazon, where there are more than 1,000 species, with many more undiscovered.

Log

Date/Time: _____

Season: _____

Weather Conditions: _____

Bug Location: ☐ ground   ☐ tree   ☐ air
☐ under log/rock   ☐ other_____

What is it doing? _____
_____

How many are there? _____

Do you see: ☐ eggs   ☐ larvae   ☐ nest/home
Describe: _____
_____

What shape/size is it? _____

How many legs?   ☐ 6   ☐ 8   ☐ other _____

If you can see eyes, what do they look like?
☐ compound (many)   ☐ simple   ☐ other _____

Any wings? If so, are they: (check all that apply)
☐ mostly clear   ☐ solid   ☐ plain   ☐ colorful
Colors: _____

Any antennae? Describe: _____

Special markings? _____

What colors are on it (other than its wings)?
_____

Name of bug I saw (enter this on your Life List)

23

56

Does it make a sound? If so, it makes a:
(circle all that apply) squeak hiss click
crackle buzz song creak chirp whir hum
Other_____

Other interesting things I noticed:

_____
_____
_____
_____
_____
_____
_____

It looks like this: (drawing or photo)

Fact

To see a praying mantis, you often have to look carefully. They blend in very well with their environment. This helps protect them from predators, such as frogs and birds.

Blending in also enables them to surprise their food, which they either ambush all of a sudden or stalk by moving slowly.

Log

Date/Time: _____

Season: _____

Weather Conditions: _____

Bug Location: ☐ ground   ☐ tree   ☐ air
☐ under log/rock   ☐ other_____

What is it doing? _____
_____

How many are there? _____

Do you see: ☐ eggs   ☐ larvae   ☐ nest/home
Describe: _____
_____

What shape/size is it? _____

How many legs?   ☐ 6   ☐ 8   ☐ other _____

If you can see eyes, what do they look like?
☐ compound (many) ☐ simple ☐ other _____

Any wings? If so, are they: (check all that apply)
☐ mostly clear ☐ solid ☐ plain ☐ colorful
Colors: _____

Any antennae? Describe: _____

Special markings? _____

What colors are on it (other than its wings)?
_____

Name of bug I saw (enter this on your Life List)

Does it make a sound? If so, it makes a:
(circle all that apply) squeak hiss click
crackle buzz song creak chirp whir hum
Other_____

Other interesting things I noticed:

_____
_____
_____
_____
_____
_____
_____

It looks like this: (drawing or photo)

Help

Avoid Insecticides
Mosquitoes aren't any fun, but if you "fog" your yard, you're not just taking out mosquitoes. You're killing all the other bugs, and it's unhealthy for humans too.

Make Your Yard Bug-friendly
If you want to help bugs, plant a "bug" garden with your family, and you'll soon see bees, butter-flies, and more!

Don't Squish Bugs!
If you see a bug inside, ask your parents to safely put it outside.

Log

Date/Time: _____

Season: _____

Weather Conditions: _____

Bug Location: ☐ ground   ☐ tree   ☐ air
☐ under log/rock   ☐ other_____

What is it doing? _____
_____

How many are there? _____

Do you see: ☐ eggs ☐ larvae ☐ nest/home
Describe: _____
_____

What shape/size is it?_____

How many legs?   ☐ 6   ☐ 8   ☐ other _____

If you can see eyes, what do they look like?
☐ compound (many) ☐ simple ☐ other _____

Any wings? If so, are they: (check all that apply)
☐ mostly clear ☐ solid ☐ plain ☐ colorful
Colors: _____

Any antennae? Describe: _____

Special markings? _____

What colors are on it (other than its wings)?
_____

Does it make a sound? If so, it makes a: (circle all that apply) squeak hiss click crackle buzz song creak chirp whir hum Other_____

Other interesting things I noticed:

_____
_____
_____
_____
_____
_____
_____

It looks like this: (drawing or photo)

Fact

Fireflies are actually beetles, not flies.

Their "flasher" can be yellow, green, or orange.

Each species of firefly has its own flashing pattern. One kind of firefly is known as the "femme fatale" firefly. It lights up with the flashing pattern of a different species, and when one of those fireflies approach it, it gobbles them up!

Log

Date/Time: _____

Season: _____

Weather Conditions: _____

Bug Location: ☐ ground ☐ tree ☐ air
☐ under log/rock ☐ other_____

What is it doing? _____
_____

How many are there? _____

Do you see: ☐ eggs ☐ larvae ☐ nest/home
Describe: _____
_____

What shape/size is it? _____

How many legs? ☐ 6 ☐ 8 ☐ other _____

If you can see eyes, what do they look like?
☐ compound (many) ☐ simple ☐ other _____

Any wings? If so, are they: (check all that apply)
☐ mostly clear ☐ solid ☐ plain ☐ colorful
Colors: _____

Any antennae? Describe: _____

Special markings? _____

What colors are on it (other than its wings)?
_____

Does it make a sound? If so, it makes a:
(circle all that apply) squeak hiss click
crackle buzz song creak chirp whir hum
Other_____

Other interesting things I noticed:

_____
_____
_____
_____
_____
_____
_____

It looks like this: (drawing or photo)

Fact

Most bugs are relatively small, but some of them are huge; the largest insects in the world are the giant scarab beetles. With names like the Goliath Beetle, there are several species that are around the same size, more than 9 inches in length, and perhaps even larger.

The smallest insect is a type of fairyfly; they get their name from their small, lacy appearance. The scientific name for one of the smallest species is even *Tinkerbella nana.*

Log

Date/Time: _____

Season: _____

Weather Conditions: _____

Bug Location: ☐ ground   ☐ tree   ☐ air
☐ under log/rock   ☐ other _____

What is it doing? _____
_____

How many are there? _____

Do you see: ☐ eggs ☐ larvae ☐ nest/home
Describe: _____
_____

What shape/size is it? _____

How many legs?   ☐ 6   ☐ 8   ☐ other _____

If you can see eyes, what do they look like?
☐ compound (many) ☐ simple ☐ other _____

Any wings? If so, are they: (check all that apply)
☐ mostly clear ☐ solid ☐ plain ☐ colorful
Colors: _____

Any antennae? Describe: _____

Special markings? _____

What colors are on it (other than its wings)?
_____

Does it make a sound? If so, it makes a: (circle all that apply) squeak hiss click crackle buzz song creak chirp whir hum

Other_____

Other interesting things I noticed:

_____

_____

_____

_____

_____

_____

_____

It looks like this: (drawing or photo)

Fact

The Polyphemus moth is famous in North America for its bright "eyespots," which are bright, eye-shaped spots on its back.

The name "eyespots" isn't far off, either. They really look like eyes, but they have nothing to do with vision. When the moth takes off, the spots help distract would-be predators, sometimes even startling them enough to make them go away.

Log

Date/Time: _____

Season: _____

Weather Conditions: _____

Bug Location: ☐ ground ☐ tree ☐ air
☐ under log/rock ☐ other_____

What is it doing? _____
_____

How many are there? _____

Do you see: ☐ eggs ☐ larvae ☐ nest/home
Describe: _____
_____

What shape/size is it?_____

How many legs? ☐ 6 ☐ 8 ☐ other _____

If you can see eyes, what do they look like?
☐ compound (many) ☐ simple ☐ other ____

Any wings? If so, are they: (check all that apply)
☐ mostly clear ☐ solid ☐ plain ☐ colorful
Colors: _____

Any antennae? Describe: _____

Special markings? _____

What colors are on it (other than its wings)?
_____

Name of bug I saw (enter this on your Life List)

Does it make a sound? If so, it makes a:
(circle all that apply) squeak hiss click
crackle buzz song creak chirp whir hum
Other_____

Other interesting things I noticed:

_____
_____
_____
_____
_____
_____
_____

It looks like this: (drawing or photo)

Activity

Take a piece of paper about 4" x 6" and go outside for 15 minutes. Find some bugs and write down all the colors you see on them.

Most will be variations of black or brown, but many beetles, butterflies, dragonflies, and moths have several colors. Some may have a colored pattern on their backs.

Try to find at least five different colors.

Do this again sometime and try to find even more colors than you did before. Where do you find the most colorful bugs? The least?

Log

Date/Time: _____

Season: _____

Weather Conditions: _____

Bug Location: ☐ ground ☐ tree ☐ air
☐ under log/rock ☐ other _____

What is it doing? _____
_____

How many are there? _____

Do you see: ☐ eggs ☐ larvae ☐ nest/home
Describe: _____
_____

What shape/size is it? _____

How many legs? ☐ 6 ☐ 8 ☐ other _____

If you can see eyes, what do they look like?
☐ compound (many) ☐ simple ☐ other _____

Any wings? If so, are they: (check all that apply)
☐ mostly clear ☐ solid ☐ plain ☐ colorful
Colors: _____

Any antennae? Describe: _____

Special markings? _____

What colors are on it (other than its wings)?
_____

Name of bug I saw (enter this on your Life List)

Does it make a sound? If so, it makes a: (circle all that apply) squeak hiss click crackle buzz song creak chirp whir hum Other_____

Other interesting things I noticed:

_____
_____
_____
_____
_____
_____
_____

It looks like this: (drawing or photo)

Fact

In the summer, you might notice huge swarms of mayflies.

In some places during mayfly breeding season, there are so many of them that they can literally stop traffic or cause accidents (as it's hard to drive through them).

Just how many are there? Well, when things get really bad, the clouds of mayflies can even be detected on weather radar!

Log

Date/Time: _____

Season: _____

Weather Conditions: _____

Bug Location: ☐ ground   ☐ tree   ☐ air
☐ under log/rock   ☐ other_____

What is it doing? _____
_____

How many are there? _____

Do you see: ☐ eggs ☐ larvae ☐ nest/home
Describe: _____
_____

What shape/size is it?_____

How many legs? ☐ 6 ☐ 8 ☐ other _____

If you can see eyes, what do they look like?
☐ compound (many) ☐ simple ☐ other _____

Any wings? If so, are they: (check all that apply)
☐ mostly clear ☐ solid ☐ plain ☐ colorful
Colors: _____

Any antennae? Describe: _____

Special markings? _____

What colors are on it (other than its wings)?
_____

Does it make a sound? If so, it makes a: (circle all that apply) squeak hiss click crackle buzz song creak chirp whir hum Other_____

Other interesting things I noticed:

_____
_____
_____
_____
_____
_____
_____

It looks like this: (drawing or photo)

Fact

When astronauts go to space, they often bring experiments along with them, and sometimes, those experiments are alive!

Astronauts have brought all sorts of bugs to space, including fruit flies, ants, silk worms, and even spiders. They did this to see how microgravity (floating in space) affected them.

On one space shuttle mission, scientists even sent an entire hive, with 3,500 bees, into space. The bees had no trouble making honeycombs!

Photo/Art

Date:_____ Description:_____

_____

Photo/Art

Date: _____ Description: _____

_____

Photo/Art

Date: _____ Description: _____

_____

Photo/Art

Date: _____ Description: _____

_____

Photo/Art

Date:_____ Description:_____

_____

Photo/Art

Date: _____ Description: _____

_____

Photo/Art

Date:_____ Description:_____

_____

Photo/Art

Date: _____ Description: _____

_____

Date:_____

Artist's Signature:_____

Color

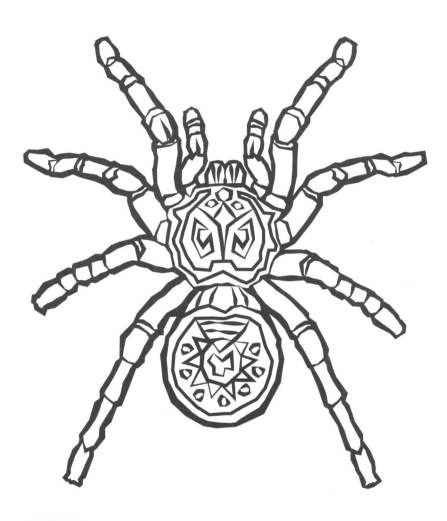

Date: _____

Artist's Signature: _____

Color

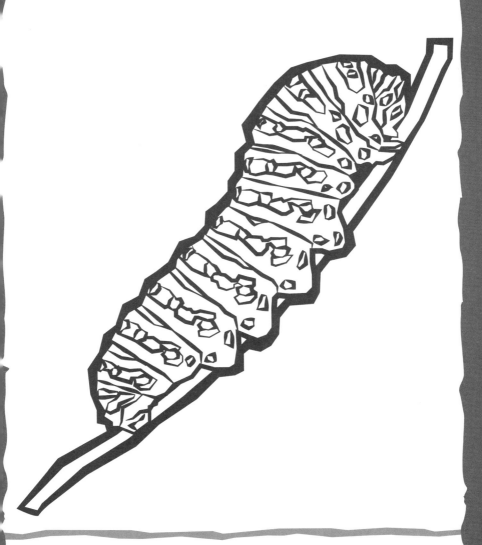

Date: _____

Artist's Signature: _____

Color

Date: _____

Artist's Signature: _____

Color

Date: _____

Artist's Signature: _____

Color

Date: _____

Artist's Signature: _____

Color

Date: _____

Artist's Signature: _____

Color

Date: _____

Artist's Signature: _____